Teaching Drama to Little Ones

JESSICA McCUISTON

A Beat by Beat Book

ISBN-13: 978-0692605370

ISBN-10: 0692605371

Table of Contents

All lesson plans are designed for a 45-60 minute session for kids age 3-7. The lessons build upon each other and are intended to be followed in order but mixing and matching activities to best suit your students' abilities is absolutely encouraged.

Introduction

The goal of this book is to empower directors and teachers with specific tools and useful lesson plans to help teach a successful theatre program and create a memorable show when working with a group of little ones (kids age 3-7).

When I first started directing children's theatre, I found it especially challenging to teach preschoolers and kindergarteners. Existing drama activities were geared toward older performers. The songs were too difficult and scripts were way too long. So I started adapting games, editing songs, and writing my own scripts. I wanted my younger students to practice valuable theatre skills, learn to be responsible actors, and perform a real show with lines and solos. This book is filled with activities that are ideal for working with 3 to 7-year-olds.

Some activities will work really well with one group of students and not so well with others. Don't be discouraged. Teaching theatre to 3 to 7-year-olds can be challenging and each group is unique. Slowly and clearly explain each new activity and then guide them through it. Don't get frustrated or feel like a failure if they don't get it. Just switch to something else and try again another day. You know your group of students the best and will no doubt make your own discoveries and develop your own tricks along the way.

3 to 7-year-olds have a relatively short attention span, so keep the class high energy and fast paced. Each lesson has multiple activities that cover specific theatre skills so that you will have plenty of ideas to work with. If you find yourself with extra time, repeat an activity that worked well from a previous class. When your little ones discover an activity they love, they will want to do it over and over again!

- Jessica McCuiston

Lesson Activity Overview

Lesson 1
Jumping Jessica
What Is Theatre?
Find Similarities
If You're Happy and You Know It
Follow the Leader
Sleeping Animals

Lesson 2
Imagination Stretching
Acting Is Pretending
Guided Mimes
Going on a Bear Hunt
Duck, Duck, Animal
Pack a Picnic Basket

Lesson 3
The Sticky Game
You're Not Alone
Mirrors
Good Afternoon, Your Majesty
Dance Partners
Noah's Ark

Lesson 4
Huggie Bear
Being an Ensemble
ABC Shapes
Machine
Streets and Alleys
Wax Museum

Lesson 5
Pass the Clap
Finding the Beat
Rhythm Leader
Boom Chicka Boom
Clockwork Marching
Timed Fairy Tales

Lesson 6
Shake Outs
Energy and Excitement
Energy Ball
Beep Beep Beep
Run a Marathon
Toy Store

Lesson 7
Jump In, Jump Out
Showing Our Feelings
Number Emotions
Sing As If
Led by the Nose
Presents

Lesson 8
Moving Day
Blocking and Choreography
Movement Leader
This Is the Way We Brush Our Teeth
Stage Directions
Do Your Chores

Lesson 9
I'm Cool Because
Pretending to Be Someone Else
Good Guys and Bad Guys
Sing Like an Angel
Shoe Game
Sculptures

Lesson 10
Baseball Game
Projection and Diction
Bean Bags
Tongue Twisters
Zip Zap Zop
Yes, Let's!

Lesson 11
Behind the Curtain
Listening and Reacting
Sensory Reaction
Nursery Rhyme Conversations
Four Corners
Walk Through As If

Lesson 12
Pass the Gesture
Telling a Story
Family Portrait
Can the Audience Hear You?
Stage Chairs
I Am a Magician

Creating a Show for Little Ones
Script
Music
Choreography

Performance Tips
Auditions
Rehearsals
Showtime Reminders

Appendix
If You're Happy and You Know It
Boom Chicka Boom
List of Tongue Twisters

Lesson 1: Getting to Know You

Objective:
Students will feel comfortable in a new environment, realizing that theatre class is a place where they can make new friends while learning how to sing, dance, and act.

Warm-Up: Jumping Jessica
- Everyone stands in a circle. Tell students to think of their first name and the letter their name starts with. Then tell them to think of a word that begins with that same letter which they can act out. It can be an action, adjective (describing word), animal, etc.
- Start with your own name as an example (mine is always "Jumping Jessica"), showing them how to do a movement that corresponds with your descriptive word-name combination.
- Everyone repeats the word-name combination while doing the movement. You may need to help younger students when it becomes their turn.
- After everyone has had a turn, start again but this time have them as a group repeat the word-name and movement for each person around the circle to see if they can remember everyone's name and action.
- This is a useful activity to repeat at the beginning of class for the first few weeks until everyone knows each other's names.

Discussion: What Is Theatre?
- Ask students, "What is theatre?" Some of them may have never seen a play, so explain how live theatre is different from watching a movie.
- Talk about how musical theatre consists of singing, dancing, and acting. Tell them that you'll be doing a little bit of all three things during every class.
- Show them where the audience will sit if you have a final presentation or show. Have them face this direction whenever possible so they get used to turning their bodies toward the audience.

Focus: Find Similarities
- The group walks around the room, looking at each other carefully.
- Say, "Find someone who has the same _____ as you" (shirt, shoes, eyes, hair, etc).
- Have them form a group with people who share this similarity and review each other's names.
- Repeat until everyone has ended up in several different groups. Explain that people can be different and the same in many ways.

Voice: If You're Happy and You Know It
- Sing the song, "If You're Happy and You Know It". Most students are familiar with it or will catch on quickly. The lyrics are included in the appendix.
- Do the standard verses, then repeat with different actions like "turn around", "laugh out loud", and "take a bow".
- These simple songs are a great way to introduce kids to singing in unison.

Movement: Follow the Leader
- Everyone lines up behind you as the leader.
- Explain that each person needs to follow the person that is right in front of them (this is a surprisingly hard concept for very young students) and not get out of line.
- Have them follow you around the room in a variety of ways: marching, hopping, skipping, tiptoeing, ice skating, flying, swimming, riding a horse, like a robot, etc.
- After the group gets the hang of it, you can select an older student to become the "leader".

Imagination: Sleeping Animals
- Everyone spreads out around the room. Tell them that you are turning off the lights (don't be scared!) and they should pretend to go to sleep.
- When the lights come on, call out the name of an animal and have everyone move around the room pretending to be that animal.
- When the lights turn off they go back to sleep. Repeat several times with different animals.
- Remind the students to use their entire body and face to become the animal.

Reflection Question:
What are the three things we do in theatre *(singing, acting, dancing)* and which one is your favorite so far?

Lesson 2: Make Believe

Objective:
Students will use their imaginations to be different characters and go on make believe adventures.

Warm-Up: Imagination Stretching
- Everyone sits in a circle and follows you in a variety of floor stretches.
- Butterfly – put the bottoms of your feet together and move your knees up and down like a butterfly. Ask students where they want to fly today and fly fast and fly slow as you pretend to go there. Then land on a flower (nose to toes) and *butterflies go to sleep.* When they wake up, ask what color flower they landed on.
- Windshield Wipers – put your legs straight out in front of you and move your feet like windshield wipers, back/forth and in/out. Reach up high for the rain clouds and pull them down onto your feet (nose to knees).
- Spider – open your legs out to the sides. Hook your thumbs together to make spiders. Have the spiders crawl all the way over to one foot, then the other foot, then all the way out to the middle (nose to floor).
- Seal – lie on your stomach and push up off the floor with your arms straight. Reach your nose up to the air and pretend to balance a ball like a seal. Then bend your knees back and try to touch your toes to the back of your head.

Discussion: Acting Is Pretending
- Ask students what they like to pretend. Explain that when we act, we pretend to be all kinds of different people, animals, and even things like trees or airplanes.
- Ask students to name places they would like to go. Explain that we can pretend to be anywhere, even places that we have never been to before.
- Give them an example of one thing you would like to be and a place you'd like to go.

Focus: Guided Mimes
- Explain that miming/pantomiming is acting without using any words or sounds.
- Have students spread out around the room and guide them through different actions that they can mime: sweeping, juggling, eating dinner, jumping rope, picking flowers, walking a dog, climbing a tree, etc.

- Then choose one student to mime an action for the group to guess (like charades). Whisper an action in their ear, reminding them to move clearly without any sound effects. Repeat with several students.

Voice: Going on a Bear Hunt
- Call and response songs are perfect for very young students. There are several variations to this one, "Going on a Bear Hunt", so use whatever verses you're familiar with. You can find all the lyrics at the link below:
  Going on a Bear Hunt: http://bit.ly/BearHuntSong
- Have students stand in a circle with their legs slightly bent and tap hands to their knees along with the beat of the song. Use as many actions and sound effects as possible.

Movement: Duck, Duck, Animal
- Just like "Duck, Duck, Goose", except students can choose any animal instead of "goose".
- Everyone sits in a circle. The person who is "it" walks around the outside of the circle and taps each student's head, calling each one a "duck", until eventually singling out one student by calling them a different animal.
- Both students run around the circle back to the starting spot, moving and making noises like the animal that was just called out.
- The student who was tapped now becomes "it" and the game repeats.

Imagination: Pack a Picnic Basket
- Tell students that you're going on a picnic. Have everyone pretend to open up imaginary picnic baskets and start deciding what to pack.
- One at a time, have each student name something to take on the picnic. Everyone should then pretend to put that item into his or her own basket. If there is an action required, everyone should do the action together before putting it in the basket (i.e. fold a picnic blanket, make a sandwich, fill up a water bottle).
- Once all the important things are packed, have everyone stand up, pick up their baskets, and walk around the room trying to find the perfect spot for a picnic. Then unfold your picnic blankets, sit down, and start unpacking.
- Ask each student to name an item that was packed. As they remember it, everyone pretends to unpack and use it (i.e. eat lunch, open an umbrella, put on sunscreen). If they forget an item, give them clues until everything is unpacked.
- This activity is especially good for preschoolers and is fun to repeat at another time, pretending to pack a beach bag, suitcase, shopping cart, etc.

Reflection Question:
How can you use your imagination this week while playing at home or with friends?

Lesson 3: Working with a Partner

Objective:
Students will build trust and gain confidence by learning to work with a partner.

Warm-Up: The Sticky Game
- Divide students into pairs and have them stand back to back with their partner.
- Tell them to try and walk around the room like their backs are super glued together and they can't ever become unstuck from their partner.
- Repeat with hands, elbows, knees, ears, noses, etc.

Discussion: You're Not Alone
- Ask students if they've ever been scared to go onstage, say a speaking line, or sing a solo.
- Explain that you're never alone while acting. There's always someone onstage or offstage to help out if you forget something or get nervous.
- Talk about having a scene partner and how it takes two people to have a conversation.

Focus: Mirrors
- Divide the students into pairs, making sure they get a different partner than they had earlier, and have them start facing each other.
- Assign one person to be the "leader" and the other person to be the "follower".
- Say, "Action!" All the "leaders" start moving very slowly, while the "followers" pretend to be a mirror and carefully copy every movement made by the "leader".
- Say, "Switch!" Partners trade roles and start again. The goal is for each pair to be so synchronized that no one is able to tell who is leading and who is following.
- Remind students to look carefully at their partner and mirror even the smallest movements like facial expressions.
- Choose a pair that you think is following each other really well. Have the rest of the class watch them, observing how perfectly they stay together.

Voice: Good Afternoon, Your Majesty
- Choose one student to be the King/Queen and sit on a "throne" facing away from the rest of the group. Remind them that part of acting is listening carefully to other people onstage.

- One student tiptoes up behind the King/Queen and says, "Good Afternoon, Your Majesty," in a disguised or silly voice.
- The King/Queen gets three guesses to figure out who is speaking. If they are unsuccessful, the student with the disguised voice becomes the new King/Queen.

Movement: Dance Partners
- Divide the students into pairs, except for one student who you select to be the "DJ".
- Play some fun dance music. Tell the partners to hold hands and start dancing.
- The DJ will tell you when to stop the music, either by actually pushing the pause button (if you trust him!) or by tapping your arm without the other students seeing.
- When the music stops, everyone runs around and finds a new partner, including the DJ.
- The student who is left without a partner now becomes the DJ and the game repeats.

Imagination: Noah's Ark
- Choose two students to step away from the group and quietly decide what animal they would like to both act out together.
- Have them move across the room side-by-side, acting like the animal they picked without using any noises or sound effects.
- Ask the other students to guess what animal they are pretending to be. If they can't guess correctly after a few tries, tell the actors that they can now use noises and sound effects.

Reflection Question:
Who can you partner up with this week to accomplish something or do something fun?

Lesson 4: Working as a Team

Objective:
Students will realize that theatre involves teamwork and everyone has a role with something important to contribute.

Warm-Up: Huggie Bear
- Everyone walks slowly around the room.
- Call out a number and have everyone group together into "hugging clumps" of that number. Repeat several times with different numbers.
- With older students, play with "outs" where those left out of the clumps sit down until the next round.

Discussion: Being an Ensemble
- Ask students if they have ever watched or been part of a sports team. Talk about how all the players have to work together to play a game.
- Talk about how we also have to work as a team in theatre. This is called a cast or an ensemble. All the parts are important and everyone has a job to do.

Focus: ABC Shapes
- Before the game starts, write out capital letters on a sheet of paper or flash cards.
- Quietly show a group of three students a letter they should form using their bodies. Tell them to work together to make the letter.
- The rest of the group tries to guess what letter they have formed. After it is guessed correctly, switch out with a new group and letter.

Voice: Machine
- Start with one student making a continuous noise and a simple repeatable gesture.
- One by one, each student joins in with their own noise and movement, until everyone is working together to create a continuous machine.
- After a few minutes, stop and ask what kind of machine they created and what they imagined their part to be.
- Repeat with a different leader, reminding them to use a different noise and movement than last time.

Movement: Streets and Alleys
- Select one student to be the "cat" and another student to be the "mouse".

- Arrange the remaining students in an equal number of rows and columns (i.e. 5 rows with 5 students in each row).
- Students should be close enough together that they can join hands with the players in their row ("streets"), then rotate 90 degrees and join hands with the people in their column ("alleys"). Have them practice switching from streets to alleys several times before starting the game.
- The cat and mouse start at opposite ends. Explain that the cat and mouse can only run down open streets or alleys, not through joined hands.
- The cat begins chasing the mouse through the "streets". After a few seconds, call out "Alleys!" and everyone switches. Change back and forth throughout the game until the cat catches the mouse.
- Repeat with a new cat and mouse.

Imagination: Wax Museum
- Everyone spreads out around the room and freezes like statues in a museum. Encourage students to creatively come up with different animals or characters.
- For the first round, you are the security guard. Walk around the room, inspecting all the statues.
- The goal of the game is for a student to tap you on the back without you seeing them move. If you catch a student moving he has to sit down until the next round.
- If a student succeeds in tagging you, or if there is only one student left standing, switch out and that student becomes the next security guard.

Reflection Question:
Do you have another class/practice/rehearsal this week where you work as a team? Remember that everyone is important and you all have to work together!

Lesson 5: Rhythm

Objective:
Students will understand rhythm, be able to clap and follow a steady beat, and practice speeding up and slowing down their voices and movements.

Warm-Up: Pass the Clap
- Everyone stands in a circle. Start the game by turning and clapping to the student next to you. The student should watch carefully and try to clap with you at exactly the same time.
- That student then turns to the next person and they clap together.
- This continues until it gets all the way around the circle. Remind students to try and keep a steady beat.
- Once the group gets the hang of it, they can choose to switch directions by sending the clap back to the sender instead of turning to the next person.

Discussion: Finding the Beat
- Ask students what they think rhythm is. Talk about rhythm being a beat that is repeated over and over, sometimes fast and sometimes slow.
- Play music with various tempos and have them clap, snap, or tap along to the beat.
- Have them make different sounds with their voices (i.e. clicking or beeping), speeding up and slowing down.

Focus: Rhythm Leader
- Pick one student to leave the group/room and wait outside. The remaining students sit in a circle. Pick another student to be the "secret rhythm leader".
- The "secret rhythm leader" starts a repetitive sound for the others to follow like clapping, snapping, or clicking their tongue. The "secret rhythm leader" changes the sound throughout the game while the others follow along without missing a beat.
- The student from outside comes back in and has three chances to guess the leader. Once the leader is revealed she then becomes the guesser and the game continues with a new leader.

Voice: Boom Chicka Boom
- This is another fun call and response song. Use different variations like cowboy, motorcycle, and janitor style. There are several YouTube videos you can watch for ideas. The lyrics are included in the appendix.
- Make sure to use lots of fun voices and movements.

Movement: Clockwork Marching
- Have students line up on one side of the room. Clap a beat and have students march on the beat to the other side of the room.
- Do it again, this time speeding up and slowing down.
- You can also repeat the activity with students hopping or skipping.

Imagination: Timed Fairy Tales
- As a class, discuss the storyline of a fairy tale or children's story ("The Three Little Pigs" is a great one to start with). Once you have discussed the plot of the story, choose a child for each role in the story. Have this small group act out the story for the class.
- After they have gone through it once, tell them you're setting a timer and they must now do it in 1 minute. After completing that task, go down to 30 seconds, then 15 seconds.
- Give them ideas or let them chat quickly in between each round about how they can cut down on time.

Reflection Question:
Do you ever listen to music at home or in the car? Clap along to the beat whenever you hear music playing this week!

Lesson 6: Energy

Objective:
Students will explore how energy is necessary when performing and learn how to control and focus that energy.

Warm-Up: Shake Outs
- Everyone stands in a circle with plenty of room in between each person.
- Students follow and count with you while shaking out your right hand for 16 counts, left hand for 16 counts, right foot for 16 counts, and left foot for 16 counts.
- Repeat with 8 counts, then 4 counts, then 2 counts, and then 1 count each. Speed up as you go along.
- Remind students to direct their full energy into each body part and not be lazy with their movements.

Discussion: Energy and Excitement
- Ask students to name a few things that they get really excited about. Explain that this excitement is the good energy that is needed while acting. Nobody wants to see boring actors who look like they are about to fall asleep!
- Have a few students stand up and give examples of having a lot of energy and then having low or no energy at all.
- Ask the other students to observe how mannerisms (facial expressions, body movement, voice levels) change as each student goes from high energy to low energy.

Focus: Energy Ball
- Everyone stands in a circle. Mime an imaginary ball of energy and squish it in your hands. While you are doing this, have students make squishy sound effects to keep the energy ball alive.
- Form the energy ball into an imaginary object (i.e. a baseball bat). Tell everyone what you have made and then mime an action with the newly formed object (i.e. swing the bat).
- Pass the object to the next person, who must then squish it back into an energy ball (while everyone makes squishy sound effects) and repeat the process.

Voice: Beep Beep Beep
- Everyone stands in a circle with heads down. Tell students that they are all aliens holding laser guns.

- Say, "One, two, three, look!" On "look" everyone looks up. If two people make eye contact, they have to point their finger guns at each other and say, "Beep beep beep beep beep…" until one person runs out of breath.
- Whoever loses has to fall down in a very dramatic "alien" way.
- Repeat until there are only two students left.

Movement: Run a Marathon
- Everyone stands in a circle. Tell the group that everyone is about to run a marathon, without moving from their spots in the circle. Remind students to control their energy so that they do not tire out before the race is over.
- Start out by pretending you're just behind the starting line and have to warm up first. Everyone follows you in stretching and jumping jacks.
- Say, "On your mark, get set, go!" and everyone begins running in place. Guide them by having them turn corners, pass cheering fans, swim through a lake, jump over a log, and any other obstacles you can think of along the way.
- Finally, cross the finish line. Have them shake their legs, drink water, and celebrate!

Imagination: Toy Store
- One student is the toymaker and everyone else freezes like favorite toys.
- Instruct the toymaker to walk around and turn the toys on and off by pressing each toy's button, turning its crank, etc. When a toy is turned on, the student must act like the toy. When it is turned off, the student must immediately freeze.
- For example, if pretending to be a jack-in-the-box, the student should crouch into a tight ball and then pop up and down after being turned on.
- Repeat with a different toymaker and have everyone choose a different toy.

Reflection Question:
What was your favorite activity we did in class today? Did it give you high energy or low energy?

Lesson 7: Emotions

Objective:
Students will explore how we use emotions to show the audience what we are feeling.

Warm-Up: Jump In, Jump Out
- Everyone stands in a circle. The group sings this song to call a student to the center:

    Group: *Jump in, jump out, turn yourself around,*
    Jump in, jump out, and introduce yourself!
    Center person: *My name is _____ .*
    Group: *Yeah*
    Center person: *And I like _____ (an activity like reading or swimming)*
    Group: *Yeah*
    Center person: *And I'll like _____ (repeat activity)*
    Group: *Yeah*
    Center person: *For the rest of my life*
- Make sure to use movement to accompany the words (jump in and out, turn around, act out their activity). Repeat until every student has had a turn.

Discussion: Showing Our Feelings
- Ask students to name emotions. Have them show you with their faces what each emotion looks like.
- Explain that sometimes we have to pretend to feel a certain way when we're acting, even if we don't feel that way in real life.

Focus: Number Emotions
- Everyone sits in a circle.
- Starting with the student next to you, have each person count off starting with "1", the next person "2", and so on until you reach "10".
- Call out an emotion or feeling (i.e. sad, overjoyed, embarrassed).
- Have "1" show an example of that emotion, then "2" express that emotion further, and so on, with each student displaying the emotion progressively greater, until you reach "10".
- Start with a different student and repeat with another emotion.

Voice: Sing As If

- Choose a song that everyone knows, like "Happy Birthday" or "The ABC Song".
- While they are singing, call out different emotions like happy, angry, bored, or surprised. Tell them to change their singing voices accordingly. Switch back and forth multiple times during each round.
- Try it first as a group and then as solos.

Movement: Led by the Nose

- Everyone moves about the room, imagining that a string is attached to their nose and it's pulling them around. Tell them they're being pulled high, then low, then fast, then slow.
- Repeat with other body parts (i.e. head, heart, hands, knees).
- Talk about how the way we walk can convey emotion, depending on if we're looking up or down, walking fast or slow, leading with our heart or our head, etc.

Imagination: Presents

- Bring in an empty box (or it can be imaginary).
- Give the box to a student and say, "Look what I got for you!"
- The student opens the box and says, "Oh, you got me a _____ (object of their choice)." Explain that they can pretend to either like or dislike the object.
- The student pretends to take the object out of the box and then shows the group how to use it (i.e. puts on a hat, throws a ball).
- The first student then gives the box to the next recipient, repeating, "Look what I got for you!"

Reflection Question:

What is something you learned in class today that you didn't know before? How did that make you feel (excited, confused, thoughtful)?

Lesson 8: Actions

Objective:
Students will use movement to learn the basic concepts of blocking, choreography, and stage directions.

Warm-Up: Moving Day
- Everyone is in groups of three. Two students stand face to face with their arms up and palms touching each other, making a "house". The third student stands inside the "house" and is the "owner".
- When you call out, "House," all the students that are "houses" break apart and form new "houses" with new partners.
- When you call out, "Owner," all the owners leave their current "house" and run inside a new "house".
- When you call out, "Moving Day," everyone scatters, either forming a new house or running inside to become the owner.
- Tell students to listen carefully to the instruction called out and not move unless the instruction applies to them. Remind them that it's very important to listen and follow directions or everything can get a little crazy and chaotic onstage.

Discussion: Blocking and Choreography
- Ask students to name different ways to get from here to there, like crawling or tiptoeing. Explain that blocking is where we go on stage and how we move when we're acting.
- Ask students to name different dance moves, like skipping or leaping. Explain that choreography is the fancy word for our dance moves.
- Emphasize how all actions should be done "full out" and not "halfway".

Focus: Movement Leader
- This is the same concept as the Rhythm Leader game from Lesson 5.
- One student leaves the group/room and waits outside. The remaining students stand in a circle. Pick another student to be the "secret movement leader".
- The "leader" starts a repetitive movement for the others to follow like swaying side to side or waving their hands up in the air. The "leader" slowly changes the movement while the others follow along without missing a beat.
- The student from outside comes back in and has three chances to guess the leader. Once the leader is revealed, he then becomes the guesser and the game continues with a new leader.

Voice: This Is the Way We Brush Our Teeth

- Sing the following song to the tune of "Here We Go Round the Mulberry Bush":

  This is the way we brush our teeth, brush our teeth, brush our teeth

  This is the way we brush our teeth so early in the morning.

- Repeat with different things we do when we get ready in the morning (i.e. wash our face, comb our hair, put on clothes, make the bed, eat our breakfast).

Movement: Stage Directions

- Briefly discuss stage history and layout: a long time ago, stages were slanted and the back of the stage was higher than the front so that the audience could see clearly.
- Tilt a book and mime with your fingers a person walking "up" stage (away from the audience) and "down" stage (toward the audience). Then explain that stage right is the actor's right and stage left is the actor's left (as you're facing the audience).
- Have students spread out facing you (the audience). Instruct them to take one step stage right, one step stage left, one step upstage, and one step downstage. Repeat this a few times, then start speeding up and switching the order.
- If they seem to understand the directions, add in things like "one hop stage right", "one slide stage left", etc.
- For older students, play with students getting "out" if they go the wrong direction. When it gets down to only a few students, have them close their eyes for the last round.

Imagination: Do Your Chores

- Call out a household chore (i.e. sweeping, setting the table, mowing the yard) for everyone to act out. Then do the action in slow motion and then do it double the speed.
- Repeat with a chore that has to be done with a partner (i.e. folding sheets, washing dishes). Everyone works together to act it out in real time, slow motion, and double speed.

Reflection Question:

If you could only move one way *(swimming, flying, dancing)* for the rest of your life, what would it be?

Lesson 9: Becoming a Character

Objective:
Students will become familiar with the practice of pretending to be different characters.

Warm-Up: I'm Cool Because
- Everyone stands in a circle with one person in the center.
- The person in the center says, "I'm cool because..." followed by a statement about himself, like "I'm wearing a blue shirt".
- Everyone who is wearing a blue shirt leaves their original spot and runs to another person's empty spot to stand within the circle.
- Whoever is left without a spot stays in the middle and repeats the activity with a new "I'm cool because..." statement.

Discussion: Pretending to Be Someone Else
- Ask students who their favorite movie characters are. Explain that the actors who play those characters are really just normal people like us, pretending to be superheroes or princesses or bad guys.
- Talk about when we're acting, we pretend to be someone else. We have to walk, talk, and even think like that character.

Focus: Good Guys and Bad Guys
- Put a piece of tape down on the floor. Tell students that one end is for good guys and the other end is for bad guys.
- Call out a character. Use a well-known one like Spiderman, Captain Hook, a vampire, a fireman, etc.
- Everyone runs to one end of the tape or the other depending on if they think it's a good guy or a bad guy. They can also choose to stay somewhere in the middle if they think the character is a little bit good and bad.
- Ask why they think each character is good, bad, or somewhere in between. Explain that each of them has their own opinion and might view each character differently.

Voice: Sing Like an Angel
- Choose a song that everyone knows.
- Tell them to sing the song like an "angel". Then after several seconds, direct them to switch it to a "giant", "baby", "sumo wrestler", etc.
- Remind them to change their voice as well as their physicality while singing like different characters.

- Repeat this activity as a solo by letting one student choose a character and having the rest of the group guess who she is pretending to be.

Movement: Shoe Game
- In this variation of freeze dance, everyone takes off one shoe and places it around the play area. The shoes should be scattered. Then remove one shoe from the play area so that there is one less shoe than there are students.
- Play some fun music and give students a character to dance like (a cowboy, an ice skater, an elephant, etc). Remind them to move around the whole space and not to dance right beside a shoe.
- When you stop the music, everyone must run and stand with their feet on either side of a shoe (it doesn't have to be their own).
- The person who is last to find an available shoe is "out". Let that player choose a shoe to be removed from the play area. Continue until there is a winner.

Imagination: Sculptures
- Divide students into pairs. One person is the "sculptor" and another is the clay.
- The sculptors mold the clay (gently positioning their partner's body and face) into different positions and shapes.
- When everyone is done, ask the sculptors to give their sculpture a name and introduce it to the rest of the class.
- Switch roles and repeat the exercise.

Reflection Question:
Who is a person or character that you can imitate really well? Try it out for someone this week and see if they can guess you are!

Lesson 10: Using Your Voice

Objective:
Students will understand why projection and diction are necessary while singing and acting.

Warm-Up: Baseball Game
- Choose two students to be partners. Have them stand far away from each other (if in a theatre, one partner stands onstage and the other at the back of the house).
- One partner pretends to throw a baseball, while at the same time "throwing" (speaking loudly) a question to their partner (i.e. "How old are you?" or "What's your favorite color?")
- The other partner mimes swinging a baseball bat and "hits" back their answer.
- Repeat until everyone has had a chance to be the pitcher and the batter.

Discussion: Projection and Diction
- Give an example of poor projection and then ask students what was wrong. Explain how, just as in the "Baseball Game" activity, we need to speak loudly so that the audience can hear us from far away.
- Give an example of poor diction and then ask students what was wrong. Explain that we have to speak clearly, enunciating all of our words, so that the audience can understand us.
- Use two students as examples and show them how to "cheat" (remind them this is the only time that cheating is a good thing!) and stand diagonally toward each other so the audience can see their faces and hear their voices.

Focus: Bean Bags
- Place three bean bags (or any other small items in the room) at three distances: the first one should be close to the students, the second one at a middle distance, and the third one far away from them.
- Have each student look directly at the first bean bag and say, "My name is _____ (their name)." Repeat to the second bean bag and then the third.
- Remind students that their voices need to get louder each time to match the distance of the bean bags.

Voice: Tongue Twisters
- Introduce a tongue twister to the class. Beat By Beat's "Ultimate List of Tongue Twisters" is included in the appendix.
- Repeat it a few times as a group; start off slow and gradually go faster. Then ask for a volunteer to stand up and say it five times fast.
- Repeat with a few different tongue twisters.

Movement: Zip Zap Zop
- Everyone stands in a circle. Have students repeat the words "Zip Zap Zop" several times as a group to get used to the order of the words.
- Tell students that you have a bolt of energy in your hands that you are sending to someone else. Clap your hands and direct it toward someone across the circle and say, "Zip!"
- That person sends it to someone else, saying, "Zap!"
- The third person sends it to someone else, saying, "Zop!"
- Keep repeating, always following the "Zip Zap Zop" pattern.
- Encourage students to clearly choose the next person by making eye contact and projecting their voice.

Imagination: Yes, Let's!
- Divide students into two groups. One group takes the stage and the other group is the audience.
- One player calls out an activity by saying, "Let's _____ (go to the mall, do our homework, go surfing)."
- All the other players support the action by jumping in and saying, "Yes, let's!"
- Everyone proceeds to do the activity together until another person in the group calls out a new "Let's _____" action.
- After a few rounds of different activities, switch groups and start again.

Reflection Question:
Is there a time this week when you can practice saying lines or singing for your family? Remember to ask them if they can hear and understand you!

Lesson II: Acting Is Reacting

Objective:
Students will understand that listening and reacting are just as important as speaking.

Warm-Up: Behind the Curtain
- Bring in a sheet, towel, or blanket to act as the "curtain".
- Split the group into two teams. A leader from each team holds up the curtain so that the two teams can't see each other.
- The leaders quietly choose one player from each team to come sit near the curtain on their respective sides.
- The leaders say, "One, two, three," and quickly pull down the curtain, revealing the two players to each other.
- Whoever calls out the other team player's name first wins a point for their team.

Discussion: Listening and Reacting
- Ask students to react when you share news like, "We're having cupcakes at the end of class today!" or, "I'm giving you a ton of homework to do before tomorrow!"
- Explain that, just as in real life, we have to listen to what people are saying onstage and react in a real way.

Focus: Sensory Reaction
- Have students sit in a circle and ask them to name the five senses (sight, smell, hearing, touch, taste).
- Then tell them to pretend they are sitting around a campfire.
- Talk through each of the five senses and how to react to them (the fire is bright, it smells like smoke, it sounds like popping, it feels hot, it tastes like roasted marshmallows).
- Repeat with another scenario like the beach, a rainstorm, or a bubble bath.

Voice: Nursery Rhyme Conversations
- Use a simple nursery rhyme like "Jack Be Nimble".
- Choose two students to stand up. The first student says the first line ("Jack be nimble, Jack be quick") any way they want (like a ghost, like a clown, like they're really sad, etc).
- The second student replies with the second line ("Jack jump over the candlestick") in an appropriate way (scared, laughing, crying, etc).
- Switch and have the second student go first and the first student respond.

Movement: Four Corners

- Number the four corners of the room.
- The person who is "it" stands in the middle of the room, closes his eyes (or puts on a blindfold), counts to ten, and listens carefully to the other students moving around the room.
- When "it" gets to ten, everyone else runs and freezes in one of the corners.
- "It" calls out a number corresponding to the corner where he thinks most of the group is hiding. All students in that corner are out.
- Continue until there is a winner. That person becomes "it" and the game repeats.
- Remind students that we have to be aware of everyone else when we are acting, not just ourselves.

Imagination: Walk Through As If

- Have students line up on one side of the room.
- One at a time, have them walk across the space as if they are in a desert, a blizzard, a haunted house, a candy store, etc.
- Remind them to react using all five senses.

Reflection Question:

How can you be a good listener when people talk to you this week? Remember to always listen carefully so that you don't miss important information!

Lesson 12: Putting It Together

Objective:
Students will learn how their newly developed acting skills fit together as they prepare for a final presentation or show.

Warm-Up: Pass the Gesture
- Everyone stands in a circle. One person starts a gesture with an accompanying sound and passes it to the person beside them. That person passes it to the person beside them, until it gets all the way around the circle.
- As they pass it around, tell them to notice how the gesture and sound naturally change. The students should not change it on purpose but just react to what is given by the person right before them.
- Repeat with a new gesture and sound.

Discussion: Telling a Story
- If you're preparing for a show, ask students to tell you the plot. Let each student add one sentence until they make it through the whole story.
- Explain that when we are in a show, our job as actors is to tell that story to the audience. They are excited to hear our story and we should be excited to tell it!

Focus: Family Portrait
- Talk about making pictures onstage and how the audience loves to see fun poses and freezes. Tell students they're going to practice this by making a family portrait together.
- One student starts by coming center and posing like they would for a picture.
- One at a time, each student adds on (sitting, standing, a hand on another student's shoulder, etc) until everyone has joined in.
- Take their picture and show it to them.
- Repeat with funny faces, like they're underwater, like superheroes, etc.

Voice: Can the Audience Hear You?
- One at a time, each student stands center stage and says a line. This is a great exercise to use if they have speaking lines for a show or final presentation.
- The rest of the group sits in the back of the house and pretends to be the audience. If the audience can't hear the student on the stage, have them

cup their ears and lean forward. If the audience can hear the student, have them stand and applaud.
- Encourage each student to repeat their line, speaking louder and louder until they get their standing ovation.

Movement: Stage Chairs
- Place nine chairs in three rows and three columns, making sure there's a chair in each of the following locations:
  >Downstage – right, left, center
  >Upstage – right, left, center
  >Center stage – right, left, center
- The person who is "it" stands facing away from the group and counts to ten, listening to the other students move around the room.
- When "it" gets to ten, everyone should be touching or sitting in one of the nine chairs.
- "It" calls out a stage location (i.e. downstage left). Anyone touching that chair races forward to (gently!) tag "it". The first person to tag "it" becomes "it" next and the rest sit "out".
- Continue until there is only one person left.

Imagination: I Am a Magician
- The group spreads out around the room. One student says, "I am a magician and turn you all into _____ (race cars, bunnies, construction workers, etc)." Everyone immediately begins acting out whatever is said.
- Repeat until each student gets a turn being the magician.

Reflection Question:
What was your favorite activity we did this whole semester? Would you enjoy doing another drama class or being in a play sometime in the future?

Creating a Show for Little Ones

Many teachers find it a daunting task to put together a show with 3 to 7-year-olds. It is challenging but it can be done! Your students will be able to say lines, sing songs, and do a few dances. Here's how:

Script

- **Simplicity** - Either edit down an existing script or write one of your own. If you're doing a musical, a few lines to tie together each song is usually enough.

- **Short Lines** - Keep each line very short with simple words and phrases. No student should say more than one sentence at a time.

- **Line Order** - Try to keep their speaking lines in the same order (Student A always speaks before Student B who always speaks before Student C). That way, they always know which student will give them their cue line.

- **Stay Onstage** - It is challenging for little ones to quietly exit and sit backstage, so think of ways to keep them all onstage and involved for the majority of the show.

- **Read Through** - Do a read through after you hand out the script. If they can't read yet, say their line and have them repeat it back. Help each student identify their lines so that they can practice at home with their parents.

Music

- **Easy Songs** - Call and response songs like "I Won't Grow Up" from *Peter Pan* or repetitive songs like "Do Re Mi" from *The Sound of Music* are great options.

- **Music Editing** - Learn to use GarageBand or a similar program (it is one of the most useful skills I have ever learned). You can cut out verses and edit songs to desired lengths that work for younger kids.

- **Group Involvement** - When teaching a new song, have students learn the entire song together, even solos. This keeps everyone occupied for more of the class time, prepares any understudies, and gives the soloist confidence to sing out when it is time to sing alone.

Choreography

- **Tell the Story** - Use simple movements and gestures that help tell the story and follow what the kids are singing. This will help them not only remember the steps, but also quickly learn and understand the lyrics.

- **Use Different Formations** - Move students to straight lines, circles, clumps, levels, and other easy formations. This will make your dances visually interesting and appear more difficult than they really are.

- **Be Consistent** - Always start with the right hand or foot to avoid confusion. Do combinations to the right and then repeat to the left.

- **Smiling Faces** - Encourage your students to smile. The majority of the time, the audience is looking at their faces, not their feet.

Performance Tips

Here are some helpful tips to guide you through the performance process:

Auditions

- **Audition Packet** - Prepare an audition packet with a short scene and chorus of a song. Email it to the parents or send it home on the first day so that the students can prepare at home. Assure everyone that the auditions are no pressure, without any need to worry or panic.

- **Audition Form** - Include a form that asks if students would like speaking lines or solos. For younger students who aren't ready for memorization yet, a group role is perfect.

- **Group Number** - Before doing individual auditions, teach a group musical number and observe who is following along and paying attention. At this age, responsible behavior is more important than amazing talent.

Rehearsals

- **Parental Involvement** - Encourage parents to review music (send home rehearsal CDs if possible) and run lines with their child throughout the week. This is especially important for students who can't read and practice on their own yet.

- **Draw Pictures** - Early in the rehearsal process, have students draw pictures of their characters. This lets them imagine what their character is supposed to look like, as well as give them ownership of their role.

- **Teach Quickly** - Run music, block scenes, teach dances quickly (remember their short attention spans!), and worry about nitpicking and fixing things later. If you get through new material fast, you'll have plenty of time to review and tighten up any problem areas.

- **Choose Good Leaders** - Keep an eye out for the kids who always know all the words and dance moves. Place them where other students can clearly see and follow them.

- **Backstage Etiquette** - This is a very hard concept (even for adults), so continually remind students throughout the rehearsal process to not talk backstage, be respectful to crewmembers, don't peek through the curtains, etc.

Showtime Reminders

- **Mind Your Own Acting Business** - Don't be bossy onstage. Never tell other actors where to go or what to do (that's the director's job), or mouth or whisper lines that are not your own. This allows you to focus on your own performance, without letting the audience know that someone made a mistake.

- **Be Smart Onstage** - On the other hand, sometimes it is an appropriate time to be a responsible actor and fix something. Pick up a costume piece that falls off, say a missed line to get the scene back on track, or gently turn your scene partner to face the audience.

- **Don't Touch Other People's Props** - This is the #1 rule about props. Props are important items and you don't want anything to get lost or broken.

- **Break a Leg!** - If you get a little nervous, just remember that you're all working together as a team to tell a story. Sometimes you'll mess up, but keep going and the audience will never know. The most important thing is to go out there and have fun.

Appendix

If You're Happy and You Know It

If you're happy and you know it, clap your hands *(clap clap)*
If you're happy and you know it, clap your hands *(clap clap)*
If you're happy and you know it, then your face will surely show it
If you're happy and you know it, clap your hands. *(clap clap)*

Boom Chicka Boom

Each line is said first by the teacher and then repeated by the students

I said a boom chicka boom
I said a boom chicka boom
I said a boom chicka rocka chicka rocka chicka boom
Uh huh
Oh yeah
One more time
"_____" style

Cowboy style:
I said a boom chicka boom
I said a boom chicka boom
I said a boom chicka rope-a chicka rope-a chicka boom

Motorcycle style:
I said a vroom chicka vroom
I said a vroom chicka vroom
I said a vroom chicka rocka chicka rocka chicka vroom

Janitor style:
I said a broom sweep-a broom
I said a broom sweep-a broom
I said a broom sweep-a mop-a sweep-a mop-a sweep-a broom

Valley girl style:
I said, like, boom chicka boom
I said, like, boom chicka boom
I said, like, boom chicka totally chicka totally chicka boom

The Ultimate List of Tongue Twisters

Unique New York

Three free throws

Red Leather, Yellow Leather

I thought a thought.
But the thought I thought wasn't the thought I thought I thought.

One-One was a racehorse.
Two-Two was one, too.
When One-One won one race, Two-Two won one, too.

Say this sharply, say this sweetly,
Say this shortly, say this softly.
Say this sixteen times very quickly.

Rubber Baby Buggy Bumpers! (Repeat. Increase the tempo.)

Silly Sally swiftly shooed seven silly sheep.
The seven silly sheep Silly Sally shooed Shilly-shallied south.
These sheep shouldn't sleep in a shack; Sheep should sleep in a shed.

Red Bulb Blue Bulb Red Bulb Blue Bulb Red Bulb Blue Bulb

Red Blood Blue Blood

I wish to wish the wish you wish to wish, but if you wish the wish the witch wishes, I won't wish the wish you wish to wish.

She sells seashells on the seashore.

Mix a box of mixed biscuits with a boxed biscuit mixer.

A proper copper coffee pot.

Toy boat. Toy boat. Toy boat.

Betty bought butter but the butter was bitter, so Betty bought better butter to make the bitter butter better.

I thought a thought.
But the thought I thought wasn't the thought I thought I thought.
If the thought I thought I thought had been the thought I thought, I wouldn't have thought so much.

How much wood could a wood chuck; chuck if a wood chuck could chuck wood.

Comical economists.

Which wristwatches are Swiss wristwatches?

Peter Piper picked a peck of pickled peppers,
A peck of pickled peppers Peter Piper picked.
If Peter Piper picked a peck of pickled peppers,
Where's the peck of pickled peppers Peter Piper picked?

Sascha sews slightly slashed sheets shut.

She should shun the shinning sun.

The big black back brake broke badly.

The big beautiful blue balloon burst.

A shapeless sash sags slowly.

Smelly shoes and socks shock sisters.

Which wrist watches are Swiss wrist watches?

Dick kicks sticky bricks.

Shave a single shingle thin.

Stick strictly six sticks stumps.

Cinnamon aluminum linoleum.

New York is unanimously universally unique.

Cooks cook cupcakes quickly.

Flora's freshly fried fish.

A bragging baker baked black bread.

Buy blue blueberry biscuits before bedtime.

She sold six shabby sheared sheep on ship.

The sixth sick sheik's son slept.

These thousand tricky tongue twisters trip thrillingly off the tongue

About the Author

Jessica McCuiston has worked as a teaching artist and director/choreographer in the New York City area since 2007. She has taught in over twenty schools, ranging from pre-kindergarteners in the NYC public school system to college students at Pace University. She currently teaches musical theatre for Bronx Arts Ensemble and Mile Square Theatre, and is resident choreographer for Broadway Bound Kids. Jessica and her husband live in Harlem with their 4-year-old daughter, who was an enthusiastic helper and guinea pig for many of the activities found in this book.

Made in United States
North Haven, CT
02 May 2023

36056039R00024